FREEDOM FROM STRESS

BY

Swami Dayananda Saraswati

Arsha Vidya Gurukulam

Saylorsburg, Pennsylvania USA

Talk 1

Looking at Our Self as a Person

There are only two things in this world: I, the conscious
self, and the objects that I am conscious of.

Most of us carry a load in our head that we need not carry.
If carrying this load is inevitable, then there is no reason for this
discussion. Since we need not carry it, then we have to find out
how to unload ourselves.

Let us look at our self as a person: Without our willing, we are a
conscious person. The self, who we refer to as I, first person singular,
is conscious by nature. The objects and various situations are what
this conscious self is conscious of.

We are conscious of external objects.

There are objects that we see like forms and colors—visual objects;
there are sounds that we hear—auditory objects; then there are objects
of smell, taste, and touch. Our own physical body is an object. Even
though we have a special relationship with this body, we are conscious
of it. So it should be taken as one of the external objects.

We have five sense organs, and there are five corresponding sense
objects. The anatomical aspect of our eyes and ears we are conscious
of. The anatomy is an object. We cannot see our eyes and ears directly,
but we can see them in a mirror. Then if we add an instrument like
a microscope or a telescope to our eyes, we can see much more
than what the naked eyes can see.

Not only what we see with our senses and with the help of instruments are objects, but the various macro and micro things that we infer are also objects (like a black hole and an electron). They are not something that we see, but we infer their presence. We can include a few more objects like the things we believe to exist. Heaven or a heavenly object is believed to exist. There is no proof, but still heaven is an object. These are all external objects.

We are conscious of internal objects.

We objectify our craving for food. We are conscious of our hunger and thirst. Hunger and thirst are internal objects. Then we are conscious that our ears are able to hear and that our eyes are able to see. In fact, we are the final authority in deciding whether our eyes see or not and whether our ears hear or not. That is why the eye and ear doctors (however objective they may be with all their instrumentation) finally have to ask us, "Do you see? Do you hear?"

It is clear that we are conscious of what the eyes see and what they do not see as well as what the ears hear and what they do not hear. With reference to the external objects, the sensory functions are internal. Only we are conscious of them; others are not. That is why we say they are internal.

We are also conscious of the various conditions of our mind and memory. We know when our mind is agitated and when it is distracted and when it does not apply itself to the job that we give it.

We are even conscious of the unconscious. How do we know that there is an unconscious part of our mind? The unconscious does not come and tell us, "I am your unconscious; nice to meet you." We infer there is an unconscious when we find ourselves acting out of proportion to the situation at hand.

When we see ourselves having so much anger over such a small thing when it is really unwarranted, then we conclude, "There is something wrong with me." Also as children, we were often told, "There is something wrong with you," which got imprinted inside.

Now others confirm it. Gradually this becomes a complex. But really there is nothing wrong.

When we were children, we picked up certain pain that we could not handle, and nature provides that certain painful situations be put into the unconscious for processing later when we are mature enough to handle it. It has to be processed later. Our day-to-day life consists not only of experiencing what is happening around us but also of putting certain difficult-to-handle situations into the unconscious. The unconscious is the flip side of the conscious ego, the self, as we know it. When we say, "I am so and so," that self.

That self has two sides—the conscious and the unconscious. We become aware of the unconscious by making an inference that our responses to certain situations are not appropriate or objective responses; there is an element of subjectivity. Therefore, there must be something in the unconscious that influences our feelings and behavior. This can be seen in all people. Each individual universally has an unconscious ego. That unconscious ego is also an object.

If all of these are objects, what really stresses you? Whatever is the source, whether the unconscious creates stress or what you are conscious of creates stress (whether the source of stress is yourself or it comes from outside), the source of stress is now reduced to an object.

When we understand the dynamics of how we function, we will appreciate that the source of stress is an object.
A parent is a source of great security for the child. In the eyes of the child, mother and father are gods. They are infallible. Whether the father is a tycoon in Texas or he is an ordinary person or he lives somewhere in a slum (the father need not own palaces and he need not be a Ph.D.), in the eyes of the child, he is infallible. He is huge in the child's estimation. "Father is infallible; mother is infallible; as long as they are with me, I am okay."

When these infallible people are found to be fallible and the child comes to understand, "My dad is not infallible," it is a big blow on that small, little head. One day father said, "I cannot do it," or "I cannot buy it," and he does things that the child cannot assimilate. Mother does the same thing because they are not infallible. They are fallible; they are mortals. They are imperfect human beings. There is a huge loss of image in the eyes of the child. The loss is not ordinary. It can be observed in the child's behavior.

Suppose the child sees a cockroach, which it instinctively knows is unpleasant and frightening. It feels incomplete and helpless and runs to the mother. Once it is by the side of the mother (in its awareness that mother is with me), the child feels complete. It no longer feels helpless. Its feeling of completeness is because of the presence and overtly expressed care of the mother.

If that overtly expressed care is not there, the child will think, "There is something wrong with me." But the moment the child finds that the mother is with it, it relaxes. The mother says, "Don't worry, I am here. I will take care of it." But then she calls her husband. He also says don't worry, but he definitely looks worried. All this confuses the child. Just think what would happen in the small mind of that child: "They are not almighty." There is a big dent in the child's image of the parents.

The self-conscious child—who had felt complete in the care, love, and availability of the parents—now begins to feel helpless and incomplete in spite of the parents. This is what we call erosion of the original trust. There was a bonding with the parents making the child feel complete, and when that bonding is disturbed and broken, the child grows with a sense of incompleteness.

The more we come to know about the world, the more we come to understand there are forces over which we have no control; there are events that we cannot avoid; there are people whom we cannot change to our own liking; and there are desires in our head that we cannot fulfill as we want them fulfilled.

4

The child finds that in strength, in skill, in knowledge, and in its control over the external forces, it is inadequate. And, as the child grows, its agenda for the external world—how and what people should be—go on growing. It is amazing! The self-conscious ego is conscious of the world and also conscious of itself as a person. So this conscious self grows with more and more agenda. The individual consists of all the past failures, successes, and agenda that he or she has for the world.

There is confusion now whether the world is external or internal. With reference to the external world, we have agenda that get internalized. Suppose a co-worker criticizes your work and you know that it is all right. If you value that person's friendship or opinion, you can internalize the judgment as, "I guess I am wrong." Therefore, when we say that the external world bothers us, it is not really the external world that bothers us, but it is the internal world consisting of our agenda for the external world that bothers us. In this instance, my agendum is to keep the friendship at any cost; therefore, I think that my work does not deserve to be defended.

This is a very important fact that we have to recognize. Objects bother us. How do they bother us? Having internalized themselves in the form of agenda, they cause conflict and stress. The objects (here the co-worker's words) need not be present at all. Even if we were to go to the moon, the feelings would be carried in our head, and they would continue to bother us.

We want the people who are closely connected to us to be different. Even as a child we wanted them to be different. But previously we had a doubt: "Are they bad, or am I bad?" If one had gone through therapy, one would definitely know that they were bad. As a child, we were helpless; we were not responsible for what happened to us. Somebody else was responsible. Generally, it is traced to the mother and father even though they did what they could do.

Previously, I thought there was something wrong with me. Now, after therapy, I know that something was wrong with my mom and baseball—it is a percentage game. We do not succeed all the time. When this is so, is it proper for me to have agenda?

Our agenda are a setup for frustration and disappointment. Please do have agenda, but understand that all agenda should be provisional. Between the agenda that we have and our self, there needs to be some space. Then only our agenda can be provisional. Provisional means temporary or conditional, tentative, subject to reshuffling. We can reshuffle our agenda. We can absorb a situation of failure without a sense of it. When we have a sense of failure, that is how stress comes. The fact is there is no failure.

When a predator misses its prey, it does not sit there and lament: "My life is useless. There is something wrong with me." That is the privilege of a human being. We have all these problems of self-judgment because we are self-conscious. But that self-consciousness can lead to a certain freedom that a tiger is incapable of because it is a programmed animal. Self-consciousness is a highly positive thing. It serves negatively only because we have not looked into the dynamics of living and interacting with the world.

One person said, "I want to run away from the hustle and bustle of this daily life and from the pressure of all these jobs. I would like to go away, give up this world, and become a swami." Where will that person go? When you live in the hustle and bustle, at least whatever hustling you have to do you do. But if you run away, there will be permanent hustle and bustle in your mind. You will feel lonely because you are not ready for that life style.

When you feel like running away from the world that means you are not ready. When you do not need or want to run away, then you can walk out. But as long as you need to run away, you had better stay. Life is a paradox. When you feel a need to run away that means you are carrying too much in your head, and that will go along with you wherever you go.

Somebody who had gone to a solitary place spoke so eloquently about it. "Solitude is so beautiful, so fascinating, so redounding to one's well being. But it lacks one thing—company." With whom? Someone with whom this person can share the joy of solitude. Paradox! You cannot get away from it because <u>you</u> are always there wherever you go.

We have to understand that every agendum that we have for the external objects has to be kept as a provision. It becomes provisional only when one is free with reference to the agendum. That means if my agendum is unfulfilled, I am okay; if it is fulfilled, I will definitely be better, but I do not rely upon that for my happiness.

This is the freedom that every human being must have. If he does not have that, life will be stressful. That cushioning space between the agenda that you have for objects in the external world and you, the person, will give you freedom to face situations where you do not fulfill your agenda.

When we truly understand that we cannot change another person, our attitude changes.
We want to be able to face situations and people as they are, but we find that we cannot but have agenda. I do not want you to give up your agenda, but you should be able to manage them, for which you require space. That space gives you a certain freedom. Freedom means you have the capacity to face a so-called failure with the attitude that it is not a failure. The attempt may be a failure, but I am not a failure. Why am I not a failure? Because it is impossible to change another person.

There is a prayer from Alcoholics Anonymous that asks God to grant us the serenity to accept the things that we cannot change, the courage to change the things that we can, and the wisdom to know the difference.

A lot of prophets and messiahs came and went. They could not change people. Kṛṣṇa was an *Avatāra* (God incarnate) according keep our agenda provisional. Therefore, we must have something more in order to discover that space. We will see that in the next talk.

- - -

Talk 2

Changing Our World View

What we want is in the form of positive and negative desires.

A positive desire is called *rāga*, and a negative desire is called *dveśa*. Both desires are called *kāma*. *Kāma* means what I want, and what I want can be positive or negative. "I want to have this" is a positive desire, and "I want to avoid that" is a negative desire. "I want to have a new neighborhood; I want to have a new house; I want to have a new job; I want to have this person as my friend." These are all positive desires.

"I want that person to have a value for my privacy and a respect for my wishes because that person is very important to me." You want a few significant people to behave in a certain positive manner. Then you want some other people to behave differently, which means they had better stop what they are doing. "I don't want him to do anything; I just want him to stop drinking alcohol." This "I want," which is in the form of positive and negative desires, is you. We have many do's and don'ts that we want people to abide by.

We want people to avoid certain things and to make an attempt to do certain things. They have to decide to undergo some change whether it is positive or negative. But we cannot change people. Parents cannot change their children; children cannot change their parents. You say those people cause you stress, but if those people were to talk to me, they would tell me that you cause them stress.

this has to be understood. For that, we have to look at the whole world from a more objective standpoint.

We found ourselves born to certain parents. We did not have a choice. Parents are given to us. Certain things we cannot change. "Given" is a very important word. Our body is given. Genetically, it has a certain characteristic peculiarity that accounts for race and gender.

The place of birth is given. It influences our life. Suppose we were born in a village in North India or in a village in South India. Those places are entirely different. The setup in which we are born and brought up for the first few years of our life is given. We do not choose that.

The culture in which we are born and the economic situation of our home, country, and of the globe are given. Everything is global these days, and for the past few years it has been like that. We were all born into this situation.

The time period in which we are born is given. The children who were born at the time of the Great Depression in America grew up differently than the children who were born after World War I and before the depression. Their value system and their attitude towards money are different. Whole countries changed after the Second World War.

It is an electronic age now, and people have too much input. What is happening elsewhere in the world happens to us. There is no more "elsewhere." If there is some upheaval on Mars, it is reported, and we know, "On Mars there was an upheaval; thank God it didn't go out of orbit or that a big chunk didn't come down on us." We get all these news items that we never got before. Now anything happening anywhere affects us.

Sitting where we are, we have to deal with all the input. Somebody is getting killed here; some people are unnecessarily destroyed there. Thus, we find the whole world affects us. That means the time period in which we are born is very important because it affects our growth, our attitudes, and our value structure.

Religion is given. When a child is born, if the parents are Catholic, the child becomes a Catholic. It is exposed to certain disastrous concepts like God and Satan—two fellows separated by a vertical line. It seems that there are Satanic thoughts and there are Godly thoughts, which are always in conflict. One is bad; the other is good. How is one going to integrate these two different concepts? What choice did one have? That is, again, given.

Education is given. What kind of school we went to and what types of friends were there was given. Some of the teachers were angry because of their backgrounds, and that anger was released on the children. Some of the teachers knew their subjects well; some of them did not know their subjects at all. That is why people in America are not shy to say, "Swamiji, I am very poor in mathematics." Everybody is sound in logic, and mathematics is nothing but logic. You simply had some poor teachers. That was given.

An unqualified mathematics teacher in the sixth grade can decide a person's entire future. Afterwards, that person will go in for history and geography because there is nothing else that he can do. That is all given. If you go back and study mathematics, you will find that you are the best. You can score a hundred percent.

My physical body is given, and that it is subject to growth and metamorphosis to become an adult is also given. My senses, their defects, and the possibility of correction is given. The possibility that they cannot be corrected is also given.

A mind that can have emotions is given. Emotions like anger, hatred, and jealousy have their own logic. It is not that we discovered how to become jealous or that we invented how to become angry. These are all given. The cognitive thinking faculty and the capacity to explore and to learn are also given.

The capacity to remember is given. And that I cannot remember whenever I want is also given. When I don't want the memory, it comes; when I want the memory, it sometimes does not come. That is given. A person at the airport talks to me as though he knows me, and I cannot remember who this person is. Then afterwards, "Oh, that is who that man is." But when I want to remember the man's name, the name doesn't come. That is given.

The capacity in my hands to develop skills like drawing, painting, sculpting, cooking, or playing a musical instrument is given. Also the capacity to desire is given. It is a privilege. The cow is not given that capacity. It is given certain programming.

Also the "not given" is given. We are not given the capacity to fly. People tell me that they feel like they are flying in their dreams, which means they have a desire to fly. But the ability to fly is not given. Wisdom teeth are given and that they are removable is also given.

The body is subject to disease and aging no matter what kind of life we live. Disease is always there, and death can come at any time. Every time we go out, there is no certainty that we will come back. That is why emergency rooms exist, and there is no guarantee that we will not wind up there. Potential danger is always there. This is all given.

Bugs are all around us and can get us at any time. Given! The immune system is given to us so that we can fight these bugs. Also the immune system can fail. Given! There are so many things in this world that can fight these bugs, and some of them do not work. Given! Finally, we have to give up. The doctor goes away saying, "This is a terminal case; there is nothing that I can do." And that person does not want to be terminated. That is also given.

The whole ecosystem is given. Water is given, and that it can be impure and polluted is also given. That there is life on the Earth and that there is no life on Mars and Jupiter is given. That the Sun energizes this Earth and that there is life possibility because of the Sun is given. The location of the Sun is given. If it were a little farther away, there would be no life possibility; the Earth would be all ice. If it were nearer, we would all be scorched. Then there are other systems and galaxies. It is endless. All these are given.

In this given world, there is a certain order. That order even includes the principle of uncertainty at the quantum level. That is also given. That the quantum objects behave in a certain manner is a given fact. The principle of uncertainty is not uncertain. We can talk about it because we are certain about it. From the quantum level to the macro level, there is a given scheme of things. This scheme of things is called *jagat*, the world. "World" is a weak word to cover all this; therefore, I will use the word "*jagat*" from now on.

Jagat, the world, is one vast order.
Jagat means that which exists in time and space and is constantly changing. It is born (*jāyate*); it is gone (*gacchati*). Born, gone, and in between changing all the time. This is what we call the changing *jagat*. It is never the same. *Jagat* means order. Stress is disorder. Anything time-bound is space-bound, and anything space-bound is time-bound. Time and space and all the time- and space-bound objects in the world constitute the *jagat*.

This is the scheme in which we find ourselves. Imagine the whole scheme is a circle. Then we are right in the center. The beauty is that everyone is in the center. Why? Because you are the one who is aware of the whole *jagat*. You are conscious of time, space, and all the objects in this *jagat*. The whole thing is given.

When I look into this given *jagat*, I see a certain fact: I see one vast order. I find that the *jagat* is order. Let us look at this order. The physical order includes all the forces. All together the weak forces, the strong forces, and the gravitational force form the order. There is a cause-effect relationship. Order! There is summer and winter. Order! There is evaporation, clouds, and rain. Order! There is time and distance. Order! Light travels at a certain speed.

Order! Even at the quantum level and the atomic level there is order.

There is as though a sunrise and as though a sunset. Order! That the Earth is spinning on its own axis going around the Sun and that it is a little bit tilted is all in order. The system itself is part of the Galaxy. Everything is moving. All mechanical actions and reactions belong to the same order. There is also a geological order. All the organic and inorganic matter that is here belongs to that order. There is a biosphere and there is a stratosphere. It is all one vast physical order.

There is a biological order. There is a frog, and from the frog only a frog comes. It can be a mutant frog, a little bit different, or one can meddle with things and produce a huge, giant frog. All given possibilities are within the order. There is a genetic connection. One has the nose of his father. All this we can see. "Are you the son of so and so?" "Yes." "You look like him."

Sometimes there is a mental problem—father was a schizophrenic, and the son is also schizophrenic. Then sometimes there is a genetic skip. The grandfather had a problem, his son was okay, but then his grandson got it. That is also given. There is an order there. Why was there a skip? There is a reason for that; research continues trying to find out why. We are sure there is order; that is why there is research. There is no simple acceptance, "Oh, that just happens; it is a random thing." Random theory is another order.

There is a physiological order. Why one is able to digest this food and is allergic to that food means there is an order there. How did one pick up these allergies? Is it constitutional or is it something that is connected to biology? Maybe it is genetic. Or there could be some other reason. We do not know what it is. "I am allergic to this" means you need not explain further. That is within the physiological order.

At a certain time, there is a metamorphosis. Afterwards, one becomes a potential father or mother. Then in one's forties, there is a decline.

The whole thing is order. This is called aging. We think we are young, but then when we read, we find we are holding the book farther and farther away. Only when our arms are not long enough do we go to an ophthalmologist and get reading glasses. That is the physiological order.

There is a psychological order. How do we know that there is a psychological order? We find in a given situation where another person is involved we become angrier than the other person. Why should we become angrier and more affected than the other person? There must be a reason for it. The situation is the same. Why do we respond in this manner? Why not like the other person? The other person seems to be okay in this situation. But in another situation, he gets angry and we are not angry at all.

It looks as though everybody has an "erroneous zone." That means everybody has "buttons," vulnerable areas, and there are always people and situations outside to push those buttons; and like a puppet I jump. Because somebody touches the button, I become angry. Even though I am a self-conscious person who can choose my actions, I seem to be delivered into the hands of something else that dictates how I behave. I react more than I act. Sometimes I act and make others react; then I again react. There is an order here also. Given a particular childhood background, this would be the psychology.

There is no sinner; there is no criminal. We cannot call a person a criminal. We can only say this person committed some crimes. Given that person's particular background, he would behave like a criminal. That means if the background were different, the person would be different.

"Given that background" means the whole behavior pattern is explainable. It means there are no criminals; there are only crimes. This is an important thing to know; only then will we stop judging people, which is important for avoiding stress. Judgment is a big source of stress. This is the psychological order.

When you look at anything that is intelligently put together to serve one or more given purposes, you construe that there must be an intelligent being informed enough to create whatever is put together, like a car, like a clock, or like the clothes you wear.

When there is such an intelligent assemblage of various things, each part plays a given role in the whole scheme. Everything has its place. All put together you call it a house. All put together you call it a car. Car means there are so many thousands of parts and so many spare parts.

All this tells us one thing. Anything intelligently put together is a product, a creation, and it implies an intelligent being or beings as the creator (it can be plural). This is something we cannot deny.

Here is a tape recorder. Suppose you ask me how I got this tape recorder, and I say I went to Japan and there, in a valley, tape recorders kept coming out of the ground like spring water. If I say this, you won't believe it. You will say, "I am sorry, Swami, up to now you were making some sense. Suddenly, what happened to you?" You are so sure it is absurd because tape recorders are not natural. They are intelligently put together.

Our physical body with all these various organs is intelligently put together. If the eyes are meant to see and they see, then they have to be intelligently put together. If the ears are meant to hear and they hear, definitely they are intelligently put together. But it is a different type of putting together, a type that a human being is incapable of.

The sense of smell, taste, touch along with the mind and the various organs like the heart, the lungs, and the entire digestive system are all intelligently put together because they function. That is what is called intelligently put together. There is so much knowledge involved at the formative stage where a lot of software programming is involved. Mother and father did not do anything. They themselves have bodies that were intelligently put together.

You cannot see a nose or eyes or any of the organs at the formative stage. But they are all there in an unmanifest condition. It is software. Wherever there is software or hardware or the connection between the two, we must know that knowledge is involved, and that knowledge is very much there.

We cannot take this physical body for granted. Every cell and every organ has a specific role to play. There is a lot of knowledge involved. Our body is intelligently put together which implies a knowledgeable conscious being as the creator. Knowledge cannot abide in inert matter. Knowledge implies a conscious being.

This implies, by extended logic, a conscious being who is informed enough—since we are talking about the world in its entirety. The known and the unknown are called entire. When I say the entire world, I mean the world that is known and the world that is unknown. The unknown world is much more than the known world. Like this flower is known to you. [Swamiji holds up a flower.] You can say this is a flower, and you can even name the flower—a carnation. But why this flower is white, not red, and why there are so many petals, and why these petals are different from the other flower's petals is not known. That is a matter for research.

There is a conscious being who put this entire *jagat*, known and unknown, together in a certain way. There is creation, there is purpose, and there is knowledge involved, which implies, by extended logic, a conscious being informed enough because that conscious being is responsible for the entire *jagat*. Therefore, the knowledge of that conscious being should be of the entire, which is what we call all-knowledge or omniscience.

There is a concept that the all-knowing conscious being is located in heaven.

Where this all-knowing conscious being is, is a thing to be understood. But instead, theologies make it into a belief. They say that this conscious being, whom they call God, is not locally around; he is in heaven. Even in India we have this concept. They will read the same *Veda* and come back with this kind of non-thinking concept. The concept is: "There is a conscious being located in heaven who created this world."

The statement "God in heaven created the world" is an expression. It can be a metaphor. It has to be understood properly. If it is taken literally, then heaven is a place. I am not saying there is or there is not a heaven. We have no way of proving or disproving the existence of heaven. When we cannot prove or disprove it, we can accept it. There is nothing wrong in that. That there is a heaven is okay, and that we will go to heaven after death, of course, is okay. But I am not ready now.

I am interested in any trip including a holiday trip to heaven. So, all right, I will go to heaven. But I do not accept that I will be there eternally. Eternity means it should exist right now. Past, present, and future is called eternal, and eternal cannot begin. There cannot be a beginning for eternity. Eternity means was, is, and ever will be. That is called eternity.

I can believe anything if it is believable. The belief in the existence of heaven is a non-verifiable belief, no doubt, but somebody said it, and I can accept it. After all, there can be a place called heaven where it is more sterile than this place. That is okay. And that we can go there for a holiday and stay for a length of time and then come back here or go elsewhere is also fine. That kind of heaven is acceptable in the sense that it is believable.

"God in heaven" should not be taken literally for it will lead to all kinds of fallacies. "God in heaven" means you are giving a location to God, which means he must be having a particular form. Perhaps he will be having a silver beard and be sitting in his own chair in his own palace. This God will definitely be a person if he has a location. If we see the front of God, we will miss seeing his back. We will not be able to see God completely. It would always be a patched-up God in our mind. Theology describes God as though he were another person like our uncle.

Children often ask questions such as who created heaven. Dad tells, "God." "Where was God before the creation of heaven?" When the answer is not known, we use authority: "Shut up. Do your homework!" Every father does the same thing. "That is blasphemy. That is a devil-asking question." Because you ask questions, they say the devil is asking questions through you. They put a devil in your head.

"Where was God before the creation of heaven?" The only possible answer is that he was in hell. "Who created hell?" "God created hell." "Why did he create hell for himself?" "That was a mistake." "Having committed the mistake, what did he do?" "Very quickly he created heaven and got transferred there and kept hell for some of us." "Who created hell?" There is no answer. The whole discussion is over.

We can always express things in different ways. The Lord in his own heavenly power and heavenly knowledge created this world. We have an expression like that in Sanskrit: "The Lord remaining in his own glory (*sve mahimni pratiṣṭhita*) created this world." That should be the meaning of "God in heaven."

To say that somebody in heaven created this world is not making people wiser. It is against all our reasoning. One can say something that is above my reason; I can believe that if I care to. But one cannot go against my reason because things are in order. There is an epistemological order.

Both the maker and the material are necessary for the creation of the world.
When you talk of a product, two causes are involved—the maker and the material. We all know that material is needed in order to make something. For example, a baker requires wheat flour in order to make bread. So the baker, using the material wheat flour, creates a product, bread. In order to create the product, the baker must have a given material. It is the same with reference to anything. In order to weave a piece of cloth, the weaver must have yarn. And

in order to spin the yarn, there must be cotton fibers. Thus, any product implies some other raw material.

I am not talking about "creationism" that the theologians are attempting to introduce into the school system. "Creation" is just a provisional word. It is not creation, really speaking. You will understand this later.

If both the maker and the material are necessary, where will the maker get the material for this *jagat* creation? The question "where" is a question asking for a location, and location means you are talking about a place in space, which means that space is an absolute existence. But this world, which includes time and space, has not yet come. Space and time collapsed long ago.

Originally, in classical physics (what is called Newtonian physics), space and time were considered to be absolute and things came into space. But that is not so anymore. Time and space are part of the creation; they are also collapsible. They, along with everything else, come into being. So the question "Where did this God find the material" cannot be asked because space is yet to come.

This is an interesting way of looking at it. Did God create the world sitting inside space, or did he create the world sitting outside space? Let us assume that he was inside space. Then the next question will be, "Who created space?" Without space, there is no question of any creation. God cannot sit inside space and create space and time; so he should be outside space. What is outside? This "outside" is itself a spatial term. Within space alone there is inside and outside.

If God cannot be outside space and God cannot be inside space and if there is a God, where should he be? If he cannot be outside, he will be inside. If he cannot be inside, then what? Perhaps space is not separate from God. That is the only possibility. Why? Because the maker cannot go for the material separate from himself.

Either the material is separate from you, or it is you. Like a spider when it makes a web, the maker is the spider and the material is not outside the body of the spider. Therefore, it is both the maker and the material.

We are both the maker and the material of our dream world. When we are asleep, there is no space, time, or encountering of the world. We do not encounter anything. Anyone who was aware of time and space is no longer conscious of time and space in sleep. Our mind, time, space, and our own individuality collapse into our self. That is sleep.

When we are half-awake, we are awake to our mind but not to our body and the physical world. We experience a dream world. Who is the maker of the dream world? Each one can say "me." Where did we find the material for making the dream world?

In the dream, suppose we have to fill up a swimming pool with water. Where do we find the water? Do we come here to the waking world and take a hose to the dream world? No! There itself we have to find a source of water. We are both the maker and the material of the dream world, and it is a "big bang." It is not that we did something the first day, and the second day we did something else.

We thought of mountains, and there were mountains. We thought of stars, and there were stars. Just in a trice, we create a dream world. For the dream world, the maker and the material both happen to be the same person.

What kind of world is this dream world? It is real for us in the dream. We don't say in the dream that this is, after all, just a dream world. No! In the dream, when people chase us, we run for our life. We have pleasure, pain, and fear in the dream. The same problems we have here are re-enacted there. The dream world is real for the dreamer until the person wakes up.

You cannot think of an object that is totally unknown to you. Never! You may say, "Swami, that is not true; I thought of a man in my dream who had horns and a tail." That is because you have seen men behaving as though they had horns and a tail, or you have seen the movie *Star Wars*. Horns, tail, and man are known to you. You put them all together because you are a creator. You thought like that, and there was this person. You can only have a dream world that is known to you. The maker and material together created this known dream world. The dream space, dream time, and dream world are not away from you, the maker, the dreamer.

There is a rule that the material and the product are always together. Together means they are identical. [Swamiji holds up a piece of chalk.] This chalk is made up of material. Without the material, there would be no chalk. There is no shirt without fabric. There is no gold chain without gold. There is nothing without the material from which it is made.

In other words, a wall that is made up of certain material does not exist without being that material. Any one thing is like that. Any product is sustained by the material from which it is made, and it has no existence apart from that material. If the knowledgeable dreamer creates a dream world out of himself (the material being not separate from himself), the dream world, including space, time, and situations in the dream, is nothing but the dreamer.

The knowledge of the conscious being, the dreamer, is manifest in the form of the dream world. Every object in the dream is non-separate from the dreamer, every object being the knowledgeable dreamer. The entire dream world is the manifestation of that knowledgeable conscious dreamer. The knowledgeable conscious being is manifest in the form of the dream world.

There is no dream world that is outside the conscious being who is knowledgeable. The truth is that the conscious being pervades the entire dream world. There are varieties of objects in the dream world, and every object is the knowledge of that conscious being.

Imagine you have created a few people in the dream. One of those people is an Evangelist who says, "God in heaven created this world." That is one theology. Another person says, "God is not in your heaven; he is in my heaven. I am the latest and the last messenger." "Latest" is to dismiss all other people; "last" is to take care of the future people who would say the same thing. That is another theology.

Another person says, "There is no God. That is all imagination. We create God out of a necessity because we are weak. In those days, people did not know how thunder came or how cyclones came; therefore, they thought there was a thunder God and a cyclone God." Some people say there is God; some people say there is no God. In the dream, every one of those people is you, and the consciousness in every one of them is the same.

There is only one consciousness that is there, and the whole fabric of that dream creation, that dream *jagat*, is within that one consciousness alone, the maker and the material being identical. The created dream world is non-separate from the dreamer. The dreamer's knowledge is manifest in the form of the dream world. You are all-pervasive in the dream. There is no dream world apart from you, the dreamer.

Just think of the faculty that we have to dream and the capacity that we have to gather knowledge and experiences for dreaming later and our senses, body, and the world where we gather all these experiences. All these are definitely put together implying an omniscient being.

The knowledge of the Lord is manifest in the form of order—this *jagat*.
The creator of a given thing is the one who knows that given thing. The maker of a pot knows that pot, and the one who weaves a cloth knows that cloth. Therefore, the maker of everything will be the knower of everything—consciousness, all-knowledge—and he is the material, too.

If you want to call God the Father, then you had better call him the Mother also. Father-Mother is our understanding of cause-effect. To extend that to the original primal cause, that cause must be both he and she. Therefore, we say that the maker is both he and she. In our Dakṣiṇāmūrti temple, the deity, Lord Dakṣiṇāmūrti, is both he and she. One part is he; the other part is she. The indication is given in the earrings. The right earring is different from the left earring.

This is not Pantheism. Īśvara, the Lord, can be without the world, like clay can be without the pot, but the clay pot cannot be without clay. Let us make it more general. The effect is the cause (the pot is the clay), but the cause is not the effect (the clay is not the pot). There is no effect without a cause (there is no clay pot without clay). In some form, the cause is there.

Īśvara can be without the *jagat*, which we call a collapsed state, dissolution (*pralaya*). The manifestation of the Lord is what we call creation. It is not a creation, really. The whole world that is here is Īśvara, the Lord. The world is non-separate from Īśvara. This is very important to know. The all-knowing Lord is manifest in the form of the *jagat*. Therefore, in every order we see, there is the knowledge of Īśvara. We need not search for the Lord.

In this manifest form, certain things are on the surface and certain potentials are there. All that we discover, like technology or anything that is created, is a potential that is tapped for which effort is required. For the purpose here in handling our stress, we require this knowledge.

The order, which is non-separate from Īśvara, never fails. Failure of the order is only in our understanding of the order. We can be disappointed and deceived by our understanding because what we thought was knowledge was not. We may have to reshuffle our thinking; the order is not going to change for our sake. There is a physical order, a biological order, a physiological order, a psychological order, and an epistemological order. All this is Īśvara.

I am a single living being with a certain individuality confined to this physical body. But within this body there are millions of cells, both native and alien. Similarly, with reference to all that is here, the total entity is one whole conscious being, which is the Lord.

When I say, "All that is here is God," this is not a belief; this is a challenge. There is nothing to believe. A belief is a judgment before knowing, and it is subject to correction upon verification. When a physicist says matter is energy, there is nothing to believe; there is something to understand. You can believe until you understand, but that is not a belief. That is what we call *śraddhā*.

Pending understanding, you believe an equation. That E is equal to MC *squared* is an Einsteinian equation. You accept it because if Einstein said it and others have accepted it, it must be true. In order to understand the equation, one must study physics for so many years. Here also when I say, "All that is here is Īśvara; the *jagat* is non-separate from Īśvara," it is a matter for understanding, not belief. We can communicate because it is communicable. That is why there is a guru. Guru means one who communicates.

The person who says, "I believe in God," does not know what God is but has some kind of a belief. There is nothing wrong in that, but when we look into the whole thing, we find all that is here is one conscious intelligent order, which is Īśvara, the Lord. It is knowledge manifest in the form of order.

This order, being what it is, the behavior of my mother when I was young was in order and even now is in order. Suppose there is a personality disorder. We are able to say there is a personality disorder because there is order. Therefore, even in disorder there is a certain order. Why? Because there is a background, and the psychological order is revealed in that background.

If somebody has a phobia, fear, that fear is due to the person's psychological background. One can probe and discover what caused

Except for mom and dad and a few others, the world consists of strangers. This is how we grow up, and we find that there is nothing but stress because we cannot relax. Stress is the absence of relaxation, and we cannot relax unless we trust. We can trust only in the infallible, nothing short.

According to certain theologies, the benevolent God in heaven loves you. The practical person will wonder, "If God loves me, why does he give me back pain? What kind of love is that?" There is an order in all this, and there is a potential. That is what we call *karma*. We have to re-establish trust in the infallible order that is Īśvara.

It is a matter of finding my bonding again. We have to re-establish the bonding that got snapped in the wake of our discovery that our parents, whom we thought were infallible, were actually fallible. We cannot bond with an inert order. Only with a conscious person can we have bonding.

In fact, that order is the conscious person, who is both father and mother. The Christian concept is of father. But that father includes mother also. The *śāstra* talks about Īśvara, the Lord, as both the maker and the material. For the sake of bonding, we say that Īśvara is both father and mother.

Only when we discover that bonding with the Lord, as understood in the *Veda*, is it possible to relax. If we can learn to relax in the awareness of Īśvara in the form of order, that is more than managing stress. That relaxation is what we call freedom from stress.

- - -

Talk 4

Bonding With God

All that is here is Īśvara, the Lord.
The fact is we have to relate to the world. It is unavoidable, and it need not be avoided. While relating, we are called upon to respond to different situations, and our responses can be objective and dispassionate. However unpleasant is the situation, we can respond without being stressed. But to be objective is easier said than done. To be objective takes a lot of understanding.

There is a psychological order in the behavior of a person. Like there is a physical order, a physiological order, a biological order, and an epistemological order, there is also a psychological order. Whether we know or we don't know why a person behaves the way he or she does, we can still understand that there is no other way possible for that person to behave at this time.

Every individual has his or her own background, and at any given time, they are doing their very best. We always worry and question, "Why did he do that? Why did he not do this?" But given the background, that person can behave only in the manner he does at this time and place. There is no other answer.

When we understand very intimately that all the significant people who bother us are behaving exactly as they can (there is no other way the person can behave), then there is no problem. And the fact is that anyone who bothers us is significant. Insignificant people do not bother us as much.

Anything that exists in time (what is time-bound) both known and unknown, including our physical body, mind, and senses, constitutes the *jagat*. While the *jagat* is not independent of Īśvara, Īśvara is independent of the *jagat* because he can exist without the *jagat*.

The rule is that an effect is not independent of its material cause. The material cause, however, can exist without being a cause. The clay can exist without being a cup, but the cup cannot exist without being the material of which it is made. This is the same truth with reference to the Lord. He is both the maker and the material cause. Like in the dream, we are both the maker and the material cause.

The truth about the material cause is that it sustains the effect. In fact, there is no effect; it is just the material cause. We have this example of a simple pot and clay. The pot is not independent of its material.

This is a very interesting thing: You are looking at the world, and in the world you want to have a vision of Īśvara. In fact, whatever you see right now is Īśvara. The seeing eyes are Īśvara, the seen object is Īśvara, and the seer is not separate from Īśvara. All that is here is Īśvara. If this is so, isn't it a foolish thing to locate the Lord in a particular place? God is called all-pervasive, almighty, and the cause of everything, and still he is located at a particular place.

All that is here is Īśvara, and Īśvara exists in a two-fold way: one way is in a manifest form that is available for our perception and interaction; the second way is as the unmanifest potentials that are Īśvara. Prayer is a special action that taps those potentials.

Prayer is the only act where our free will enjoys total freedom. In all religious cultures, prayer is common. Prayer can be in any language and in any form. The Lord does not have a linguistic problem. He can be invoked in Hindi, Latin, Greek, French, Hebrew, English, or an Arabic language. This is not the same as saying all religions lead to the same goal. They do not! When I say all that is here is

Īśvara, what is here you have to claim, and you claim that through prayer. If you do not claim it, then you are the loser.

All prayers are valid. Prayer is an action (*karma*) because it stems from you as a doer (*kartā*). Anything that stems from you, a doer, is called action. It comes from your free will. The human free will is difficult to define because we do not know which is free will and which is pressure. In all actions, some free will is involved. But more often than not we find we are in a corner where we are constrained to do an action. Therefore, we do not know how much freedom that free will enjoys. It is disputable.

There is always pressure, inner pressure and outer pressure. Outer pressure finally becomes inner pressure when somebody pressures you and you internalize that situation. If you refuse to get pressurized, there is no inner pressure; there is only outer pressure. The pressure is for the other person; it remains his agendum, not yours. When you internalize the other person's demands, it becomes your duty or your pressure; you feel you have to do it.

Due to pressure, one is constrained to do certain things. Even a reaching-out action like charity is sometimes done because of our own empathy. When we see somebody in pain, we pick up that pain. That is human nature. First, we empathize; then, in order to eliminate that empathy, we do something that sometimes becomes a reaching-out action. There again there is pressure that is empathy born.

Social service is empathy born. However, some people do social service with an agendum for converting people. For all the eyes that see the work, it looks like service; but the person has a certain plan, a program to convert the people to a different religion. Therefore, that is not considered service. That is only a means for accomplishing an end. The means happens to be good, but the end is not good because a culture is being destroyed. It is not necessary.

Perhaps a person is really reaching out to help someone. Without receiving any monetary reward whatsoever, one does an action.

However, nobody does anything without expecting some kind of a reward, and there is always some reward for anything that one does. Perhaps the person is getting rid of his or her empathy-born pain, or maybe the reward is discovering the joy in sharing. So even a reaching-out action is a pressurized action. One's own empathy pressurizes one into doing something.

Prayer is the only action where our free will enjoys total freedom. We need not pray. "But, Swamiji, it is a prayer in distress; I am in a difficult situation." But in distress you need not pray. In distress, you can hit your head on the wall. In pain and in distress, you can do a hundred different things. You can take alcohol; you can take drugs; you can go on a buying or killing spree. You need not pray. Why? Because you do not see an immediate result.

Prayer has two results. An immediate result and an unseen result. The unseen result of prayer is called *adṛṣṭa phala*. It will manifest in time and is what we call grace. It is produced by an action and accrues to the doer of the action, the one who prays. This is a potential, and the potential you tap. Like there is underground water that has to be brought out by a series of actions. So also prayer is an action tapping the potential grace. The immediate result of prayer is called *dṛṣṭa phala*. That you can pray is itself an immediate result. It is not easy to sit and pray.

A prayer can be said in simple words, or it can be an elaborate ritual, or it can be purely oral or purely mental. Prayer can be described as three different forms of action—physical (*kāyika*), oral (*vācika*), and mental (*mānasa*). A ritual is a physical form of prayer; singing in praise of the Lord is an oral form of prayer; and chanting a *mantra* silently is a mental form of prayer.

When we act, our intention becomes complete. When we want to wish somebody a happy birthday, we can just mentally think about that person and wish the person well and that is all. But when we take the time to choose a card, buy it, write something on it, and then post it, our wishes become totally manifest. When we act it out, our intention is fulfilled.

That is why we have a daily ritual as a form of worship. The ritual is performed at an altar where flowers, incense, and light are offered. This is purely cultural. Nobody worships an idol. People worship only the Lord, and the Lord being everything (there is nothing outside him) every form is the Lord's form. In any form that you recognize as Īśvara, you can invoke the Lord. It is purely invocation. When we invoke the Lord at an altar and offer worship, it is called *kāyikam karma*, which involves the physical limbs, the mind, and the organ of speech.

Oral prayer, *vācika karma*, is common in all religious traditions and is also there in the Vedic tradition. It involves the mind and the organ of speech. The same prayer can be mental, which is called *mānasa karma*, involving the mind alone. It is called meditation, a mental activity for which the object is *saguṇa Brahman*, Īśvara, the Lord.

We bond with Īśvara by doing actions that invoke the devotee in us.
While doing these prayers, we are producing an unseen result called *adṛṣṭa phalam*, which makes the difference between success and failure. It is called grace. But more than that, the devotee is invoked in us. We need to establish a bonding with Īśvara, a bonding that got snapped between our parents and us.

We started our life with complete trust in our parents. As we grew, we naturally took our mother and father to be infallible. That bonding that was there was with the almighty infallible, and our father and mother constituted that almighty infallible God. As a child, we did not have any other God except these two people.

Afterwards, when we discovered that our parents were not almighty but they were fallible, that trust faded. The infallible parents became fallible in the eyes of the child, and the bonding was snapped. Then all our lifetime we have been searching for the infallible. There is a longing to bond with a being we can trust. That bonding has to again be established.

This is an enlightened bonding. In the baby, it was an innocent bonding. Understand the difference. Here we have grown up in our life, and we understand what Īśvara is. The bonding that is established now is deliberate bonding by knowing, first, this is Īśvara, and then by doing such actions that establish that bonding, actions that will invoke the right person in us. A person who has that bonding will never have stress.

Suppose you are jealous of somebody with whom you have to live, and you want to remove this jealousy. Jealousy is the pain born in the wake of knowledge that somebody is happy when you are not. Once jealousy comes into the mind, it grows and the only cure for it (if at all there is one) is to do something. You have to act it out in the opposite way. Give the person a rose every day for forty days. Tell him, "I want to get rid of my jealousy, so please accept this rose." When you are honest, people are different.

Your commitment to change is manifest in that action of giving a rose to that person to whom you would rather not give a rose. It takes a lot of commitment to change. Definitely, it is a deliberate action. Only by acting it out, as though you already have the quality you are seeking, do you change. You fake it till you make it. We do this all the time. How did you learn swimming? By faking it and making it. You have to enter into the water and swim. The swimming teacher tells you, "Come on, swim! Do the same thing as I do." In the process, you learn swimming. You learn driving by driving. You learn cooking by cooking. You learn everything by doing it. There is no other way.

We have to establish bonding with Īśvara. Once that bonding with Īśvara is there, we can relax. As we saw before, when a child feels insecure and afraid because something like a cockroach is seen, it runs to its mother. Once it is standing near its mother, it feels safe because it trusts that the almighty, infallible mother can take care of it. The child feels powerful now.

Then that trust is eroded when the mother calls dad. The child thinks that dad is almighty and infallible, but then dad cannot handle the situation either. So from this the child quietly understands that they are fallible. First, a vague understanding is there. Then the clarity grows as the child grows. Afterwards, the bonding is gone. One has to become complete again.

As a child, we were together with our mother before birth, and that connection was snapped after delivery. Then we seek that bonding in life that can take place only with the infallible. That is why people love a religion that has a savior. That is why those religions that have a savior to offer have followers, and that is also why there is savior psychology. Thus, all the cults come into the picture because people want somebody to save them.

Human beings are fallible in the sense that they are limited in knowledge, strength, and power. Only the total conscious being is infallible. The order itself is the conscious being, the order being not separate from the conscious being. Īśvara is the infallible; the order is infallible.

If I find the order is fallible, it is not the order that is fallible, but my understanding of the order that is wrong. The order can never disappoint me. It is my expectation that disappoints me. And that is to be expected because my knowledge is limited.

The devotee in us is the basic person who plays different roles. The basic person is always relaxed. Between the basic person and the role that the basic person is called upon to play, there is always a distance, and the distance is the awareness of the basic person.

To one person, we are related as a son or a daughter. To another person, we are related as a husband or a wife. To another person, we are related as a father or a mother. To another person, we are related as a brother or a sister. To another person, we are related as a neighbor, as a friend, and so on. The person being the same, the roles vary.

I, the subject, am the same. Therefore, I am father, I am son, I am husband, I am brother, I am wife, I am mother, I am daughter, I am sister. *I am* is constant in all this, but whom I relate to is variable. I am always there in all the relationships. Therefore, I am constant. But am I totally constant? No! There is a certain variable component there also.

To my father, I am son. But to my son, I am father; and to my brother, I am brother. That means what? Not only are the people different, I am also different. I am son, I am father, I am brother. It is clear that I am also changing. However, there is also an invariable element in this. *I am* is invariable.

I am is the basic conscious person (*puruṣa*), not male or female. This is what we are, and this conscious person is playing different roles like father, son, and husband. Some roles are a little difficult to play, but still they are roles. I am father with reference to my son or daughter; I am son with reference to my parents.

Each role is a status that I assume depending upon the relationship. This is how we are all cast in life. The world is a stage, and we are all players playing different roles, and every role has a script that becomes evident according to the situation. Nobody has to write the script. We all know exactly what we have to do, and if we do not know, we can ask somebody. We can follow this script meticulously and happily if we know, "I am the basic person playing the role."

Imagine an actor playing the role of a beggar. The actor is on the stage now; and, according to the script, he has to undergo a lot of pain. People abuse this beggar, and he has to suppress his feelings and still go about begging. Now and then he has to cry. He is happy because he is shedding real tears. The tears just roll down his cheeks. The people in the audience are also crying.

He is congratulating himself: "I am doing very well." Not only he thinks he is doing well, but a friend, who is sitting in the audience, also thinks he is doing well and comes backstage to congratulate him: "Hey, you did wonderfully. How did you manage to cry like that?" However, while crying even more the next day because he lost a loved one, if the same friend were to say, "Hey, you are crying even better today, congratulations!" that would be inappropriate. That was a role; this is real.

Let us look at that role. The actor was congratulated for his crying. He was also self-congratulating. How come? Because he is not the role. There is a cushion of understanding "I am not the role." The actor is not the beggar even though the beggar is the actor. The role's body is his body; the role's mouth is his mouth; and all the words in the script are from his tongue. Therefore, the beggar is totally the actor, not just partially the actor (there is no distance by time between the actor and the beggar), but the actor is not the beggar. (B is A; A is not B.)

The beggar is suffering; the actor is not suffering. The beggar's suffering is confined to the beggar, not because the actor is different but because the actor is not the beggar. So understanding that the beggar is the actor but the actor is not the beggar is the cushion. That knowledge gives us the space to play the role according to the script and enjoy playing it also.

We find ourselves in a given setup in a vast universe where there are a few significant people whom we would like to change. Those significant people bother us, and related to those people we are playing various roles. But in real life, we don't look at it as playing roles. We assume that on the stage it is a role, but offstage it is not a role. However, "offstage" is also a stage.

The drama of life has to be understood. Shakespeare had a great mind and somehow felt all this without Vedānta because the truth is the same. He understood the emotions of the human mind very well, and he had a way with words. As someone said, Shakespeare's mind is the platform of the world. He said, "The world is a stage; all men and women are but players," which is true.

My relationship with Īśvara is basic, fundamental, and invariable. When I relate to my grandfather, I am grandson. When I relate to my father, I am son, not grandson. In order to be a son, I replace my grandfather with my father. My relationship with the Lord is not the same. As an individual, I am fundamentally related to the Lord whether I recognize the relationship or not. This relationship is expressed by the word "devotee."

As a devotee, when I assume the role of father or son, the devotee is not replaced. This relationship between the Lord and me is the same as that between my father and the Lord or my friend and the Lord. The devotee remains due to the abiding nature of the relationship with the Lord.

First and last, I am a devotee connected to the total, to Īśvara. I am a conscious being; Īśvara is a conscious being. That particular relationship is basic, fundamental, and invariable. Therefore, when I am a father or a mother, I am that basic person, the devotee. I am a devotee father, a devotee mother, a devotee husband, a devotee wife, a devotee son, a devotee neighbor.

Awareness of my being that basic person, the devotee, is a cushion, a space that gives me the freedom from being stressed by playing a role. We cannot avoid playing roles just so that we can avoid stress. We have to play our roles. If you list all the problems you have, you will find that all the problems belong to the roles.

As a father or mother, daughter or son, husband or wife, you have some problems. All these problems are the role's problems, not the person's problems. Where is stress I would like to know? Is there any drama without plots and without changes? There is no drama in life without plots. All that must be there. Real life is like that.

There are very quick turns. Shakespeare was famous for those turns. Everything is going well; then suddenly everything changes. The drama of life has to be understood as such.

As an individual, I see myself as a devotee. A relationship that exists with Īśvara is recognized. As a devotee, I invoke the help and the grace of the Lord by an act of prayer. Prayer is an action. The result is what is called "grace." I create grace through the act of prayer; and, also, through the various forms of prayer, I establish my bonding with Īśvara.

The significant people that are in the cast of our life may make some omissions and commissions. Sometimes there are omissions and commissions on our part also. A good actor makes up for all the omissions and commissions and keeps the drama going and makes it enjoyable, too.

* * *

BOOKS BY SWAMI DAYANANDA

Action and Reaction
Bhagavad Gita Home Study Course (780 pages in 2 binders)
Crisis Management
Day after day with Swami Dayananda
Dialogues with Swami Dayananda
Emotional Maturity
Freedom from Fear
Freedom from Sadness
Fundamental Problem
Introduction to Vedanta
Morning Meditation Prayers
Personnel Management
Problem is You; The Solution is You
Purpose of Prayer
Sadhana and Sadhya (The Means and the End)
Sri Rudram (1 book + 1 tape)
Talks and Essays of Swami Dayananda
Teaching of Bhagavad Gita
Teaching Tradition of Advaita Vedanta, The
Two Talks on Japa: Mantra Meditation
Upanisads and Self-Knowledge, The
Value of Values
Vedantin's View of Christian Concepts, A
Who Am I?

Please contact:
Arsha Vidya Bookstore,
P.O. Box 1059,
Saylorsburg, PA, 18353

(570) 992-2339 Ext. 223 · Fax (570) 992-9617
http://books.arshavidya.org